Sandy's new home

by *Sylvia Root Tester*
illustrated by *Sher Sester*

THE CHILD'S WORLD

ELGIN, ILLINOIS 60120

Library of Congress Cataloging in Publication Data

Tester, Sylvia Root.
    Sandy's new home.

    (Handling difficult times)
    SUMMARY: Resentful of the move that is taking
her far away from her friends and familiar surround-
ings, Sandy decides to run away.
    [1. Moving, Household—Fiction.   2. Family life—
Fiction]   I. Sester, Sher.   II. Title.   III. Series.
PZ7.T288San   [Fic]   79-15923
ISBN 0-89565-098-3

Distributed by Childrens Press, 1224 West Van Buren Street,
Chicago, Illinois 60607.

Sandy's new home

I won't stay! Sandy thought. They can't make me! Once we're there, I'll wait awhile. And then I'll run away! Sandy had been trying not to cry all morning. She was still trying.

The car moved steadily down the road toward their new home. Sandy pulled her legs up and wrapped her arms around them.

Her brother Ron sat in the other corner of the back seat. He was mad at her because she wouldn't play his silly game with him. But they'd played it for two days. That was enough. Sandy was bored with it, bored with this whole dumb trip. She was tired of restaurants, tired of motels.

She was especially tired of Great-Grandmother Pierce, who complained about everything she did. And she was especially tired of little Mindy, who got loved every time she cried.

Ahead of them, the big, rented, moving van signaled a right turn. So Sandy's Mom put on her turn signal too. The truck and car pulled into a parking lot.

"Time to eat," said Mom. She shook Great-Grandmother Pierce awake. Sandy, Ron, Mom, and Grandma got out of the car. Dad and Mindy got out of the truck.

"I got to ride in the truck!" Mindy yelled. "Grandma, I got to ride in the truck!"

Grandma patted Mindy's head. "You sure did, Honey," she said.

"Big deal!" Sandy said, under her breath. But Great-Grandmother Pierce heard. She frowned at Sandy.

Dad took Grandma's arm. "This is too long a trip," he said.

"Think I can't make it?" Grandma snapped.

"Did I say that?" asked Dad.

Grandma mumbled something as she went in the door to the restaurant, holding Mindy's hand. Dad shot a glance at Mom, who shrugged.

"She's always grouchy when she wakes up," said Ron. "That's all it is." Mom smiled and put her hand on his shoulder.

Suddenly Sandy felt all alone. "She's always grouchy, period!" she said loudly.

"Like someone else I know!" said Ron.

"Sandy," said her mother, "let's take a walk around the parking lot before we go in. We need the exercise." She motioned Ron on into the restaurant.

Uh-oh! thought Sandy. Here it comes!

"Hon," her Mom said. She brushed Sandy's hair back from her face, then put an arm lightly around her shoulder. "I know this is a long trip. Three days in the car." They began to walk. "But things will be better in our new home."

"I don't see how!" said Sandy.

"Well, for one thing, Dad has a much better job. For another, you won't have to share a room with Grandma. She'll have her own section of the house. That's the best thing about our new house."

"I'll just have to share with Mindy!"

"That's worse?"

Sandy knew it wasn't. "It's no better! she grumbled.

"Sometimes, Sandy. . ." Mom shook her head. "Sometimes you sound downright cranky!"

"I do not!" Sandy pulled away. "You just don't like me! You want me to lose all my friends! I'll never see Anne again, or Maria, or Joe, or any of them! And you don't care! You did it on purpose!"

"Sandy!"

Sandy could see that she'd hurt her Mom, but she didn't care. She ran back to the car. She climbed in and locked all the doors. She huddled in her corner.

Her mother sort of threw up her hands. Then she hurried into the restaurant.

"I won't get out of this car!" Sandy said. "I won't!"

But no one came to make her get out.

Sandy found her paper and a pencil. "I am going to run away!" she wrote. It was a note to herself, a promise. She folded up the note and put it in her shoe.

Still, no one came to make her get out.

Sandy looked over at the restaurant. All of them were there, right by the window. Grandma looked out and frowned at Sandy. Mindy waved to her. Ron put his hand up, so no one could see his face. Then he stuck his tongue out and laughed. But Mom and Dad didn't even look toward the car.

Sandy lay down on the seat so she couldn't see any of them. "I'm not gonna cry!" she said. "They don't even care!"

But the tears came anyway. Sandy cried and cried, until she fell asleep.

Sandy woke up to see her Dad bending over her. "Come on, Love," he said. "Your turn in the truck."

"You spoil her," said Grandma. "After a tantrum like that. . ."

"Grandma!" said Mom. "Leave her alone! All of us are tired and grouchy from the trip!"

"Well!" said Grandma, but that was all.

When Sandy got in the truck, her Dad slid a hamburger and some milk toward her.

"Thanks," she said. She was suddenly very hungry. She settled down to eating.

"Feeling better?" her Dad asked.

Sandy nodded. "Does Grandma know you brought me food?"

Her Dad grinned. "No. I sneaked around."

Sandy grinned too. "Bet she wouldn't like it."

Dad shrugged. "She has different ways. She thinks children ought to behave or be punished. No matter what. And sometimes, she's right. So don't be too hard on her."

"She just doesn't like me. That's all!" said Sandy. "She never has! Why doesn't she like me?"

Her Dad shrugged again. "Why don't you like her?"

"Because she expects me to be perfect all the time! Pick up that toy! Pick up that sweater! Make that bed! And it's. . . it was. . . my room! And she snores!"

"Maybe she has the same problems with you," said Dad.

Sandy looked over at him. Was he kidding? She couldn't tell. "I don't snore!" she said.

"How do you know?"

"I just do!"

"Well," he said. "There may be some things you don't know."

"Like what?"

"Great-Grandma Pierce had a whole house, all to herself, before she came to live with us. With us, all she had was half of your room. That's hard for an old woman.

"Besides that, she has arthritis. Sometimes it hurts her, really bad. It hurts her to bend over. It even hurts her to sit down in a chair."

"I guess I didn't know that," said Sandy.

"Was it so terrible. . . sharing with her?"

"Yes!"

"All the time?"

"Well, most of the time."

"Three-fourths?"

Sandy thought. "At least half the time."

Her Dad didn't say any more. He just smiled.

.   .   .

Late that afternoon, Dad said, "Well, here we are." He parked the truck in front of a large, old house. Sandy got out and stood looking at it. It seemed to go up and up and up.

"It needs some work," Dad said, "but it gives us a lot more room."

Sandy knew her Dad wanted her to say something, but she didn't know what. He shrugged finally and went to open the door.

The next few hours were very busy. They had to get everything into the house.

Some kids from down the block came to watch. One girl talked to Sandy a little. Sandy thought maybe she'd like her.

Then it was time for supper—chicken from a carry-out. And the work began again. Finally, all the furniture, all the boxes, all the bags were inside the house.

"That's it for tonight!" said Dad.

Sandy looked around her room. It was a large, large attic room. Her bed was here. Her toy box was here. Her clothes were here. Most of the things were still in boxes, but they were here.

A bookcase divided the room in two. Over on the other side, Mindy was already asleep.

Sandy reached up and touched the sloping ceiling. Her mom had said they'd put wallpaper on the walls and even on the sloping ceiling. And Sandy could pick out the wall paper, 'cause Mindy was too little.

Sandy walked over and looked out her window. The tree branches just outside moved gently in the breeze.

"It's like a tree house, here at the window," Sandy said softly. She looked down, down, down to the street. She could see the whole block from that window. Sandy stood looking out. Then she took a deep, deep breath.

She decided to make a last tour of the house before going to bed. She came down the steps quietly. Ron was putting his car collection out on his dresser. "Look," he called, "there's room for everything!"

Sandy stopped to let him show her. "He's O.K. here," she decided.

Sandy went on down to the ground floor. Her Dad had stretched out on the couch to read a magazine. He was sound asleep.

"Just like at home," she whispered. She went through the living room and kitchen.

Grandma's three rooms were there, off the kitchen. Sandy could hear Grandma and Mom talking inside. Timidly, she knocked.

"Come in," said Grandma. Sandy opened the door and stepped inside.

"Well," said Grandma, "two visitors in my little home, and on the very first night. Come, Sandra, have some herb tea."

"Can you imagine?" said Mom, smiling. "Grandma has managed to heat water. The stove isn't even hooked up. But she found her electric coffee pot and her tea. And in all this mess, she even found her china tea cups!"

Sandy took the hot cup of tea and sipped it. It tasted of orange and spice. "It's very good," she said. "Thank you."

Grandma beamed at her. Sandy drank her tea and listened as the two women talked. They seemed to have forgotten she was there, which was all right with her. Grandma was so pleased with her three rooms. Sandy couldn't remember ever seeing her so happy.

Mom's right, Sandy thought. Grandma's separate part is the very best thing about this house. It's already home to her.

Finally, Mom said, "Well, Grandma, Sandy and I must go to bed. Thank you for the tea. It was just what I needed."

"Sandy," said Grandma as they walked to the door, "if you get tired of Mindy bothering you, you can always come and visit me."

"O.K." said Sandy, "and if you get tired of being alone, you can come and visit me."

Grandma nodded. "That's a fair trade."

.   .   .

As Sandy took off her shoe, she saw the note to herself, about running away. She opened it and read it.

"That was silly!" she said. She tore the note in little pieces and stuffed it in the trash.

"I think I want green wallpaper," Sandy said. "Soft green. Yes, that's perfect for a tree-house room."

In no time at all, Sandy was sound asleep, safe in her new home.

THINKING AND TALKING

The story in this book begins in the middle. Sandy and her family are already on their way to a new home. What do you think happened before this story began?

How far ahead might the family have known about the move? How would they have gotten ready? Who would have done the packing? Do you think Sandy helped? What about Ron? Would Mindy have helped?

There is much, much work to do when a family moves to a new home. First, the old home may need to be sold—if the family owns it. Then the family must sort through all the things in the house.

Some things get thrown away. Sometimes a family has a sale and sells some things. Sometimes, some of the things are given away. Sometimes the family takes almost everything they have along with them to the new house.

Parent's have to take care of many details. They go to the post office. They tell the people there what their new address will be. They call the electric company and gas company. They call the phone company. They have many, many other things to do, too. It seems as though they are busy, busy, busy, all of the time. This sometimes makes it hard on children. Their parents are so busy, it's hard to talk to them.

Moving is often sad. Children are sad because they are leaving good friends. And they are sad because they are leaving a familiar place. Sandy had to leave her school. She had to leave the park she loved, near her house. If you moved, what would you have to leave? What would you miss most?

Sandy became very tired and very angry and

upset. How could you tell she felt this way? What would you have done if you felt that way? Children often become angry and upset during a move. So do adults. It is a hard time. Everyone is tired. Everyone is grouchy. Did Sandy's parents understand how she felt? How do you know? Yes, they didn't punish Sandy for talking and acting as she did.

Do you think Sandy's parents felt sad about the move? Would your parents feel sad if your family moved? Most people, even grown-ups, do feel sad. Sometimes grown-ups don't show their sadness as much as children. That's because they have to be in charge. They have to get everything done.

There is another reason parents don't seem so sad. They usually know the new place will be good, as good as the old place. They have moved before. But children don't know this.

They don't find this out until it happens.

At the end of the story, how did Sandy feel about the new house? What did she like about it? What did she do to get used to the house?

How did Great-Grandma Pierce feel about the new house? How do you know? How did Sandy's parent's feel? How do you know? How did Ron and Mindy feel? How do you know?

Have you ever moved? How did you feel about moving?

Often, children are fearful about moving. They don't know what to expect at the new place. They wonder if they will like the new house or apartment. They worry about meeting new people. They worry about the new school. It's normal to be a little fearful about moving.

One thing is helpful to remember, if you are

moving. You liked your old home. That means you can learn to like your new home. It might even be better. You have made friends before. That means you can make friends again. They might even be better friends. You got used to one school. That means you can get used to another school. It might even be a better school. These things take some time. They won't be easy. But they will happen. If you did these things once, you can do them all again.